FLY FISHING
KNOTS & RIGS
LEADERS

TREVOR HAWKINS

Published and distributed by
Australian Fishing Network
48 Centre Way, Croydon South, Victoria 3136
Telephone (03) 9761 4044 Fax (03) 9761 4055
Email: sales@afn.com.au
Website: www.afn.com.au

Contents

Introduction

It was never my intention to compile and illustrate a book on knots and rigs. It all started with a few illustrations of knots for another project. When Bill Classon saw them, he said, as he often does, "Let's do a book."

The next statement went something along the lines of, "A book on fly fishing knots, of course you will have to illustrate another twenty or so knots. Oh, by the way, it can't just be about knots, let's do some rigs and leader recipes also."

So there you have it. Of course the other project was put on hold for the next two months while this little book was put together. Apart from working to a deadline, I've enjoyed the experience immensely. I've found it very interesting to evaluate knots and rigs for inclusion into this book, after 37 years of fly fishing you tend to get set in your fishing ways, you have your favourite waters, both at home and overseas and you have your favourite knots and rigs.

I've included many knots that I haven't used for some years. It's not that they are ineffective, it's simply because the type of fly fishing I now do doesn't require those knots. Compiling this book has made me think about the knots and rigs that I tend to use over and over again on my favourite waters, and question whether or not I should go back to some of my older favourites. All of the knots in this book other than perhaps the Turle Knots, (which I have included purely from an interest point of view) are relevant for today's fly fishing needs.

Tie and try the knots and rigs that are most suitable for your fly fishing needs and perhaps add a few extras to your repertoire. Knots may not be the part of fly fishing that gets you excited, but it is one area where you should strive to be proficient. It really can mean the difference between a good and a bad day on the water.

I hope that you get as much enjoyment and information out of this book as I did in putting it together.

Trevor R. Hawkins.

Conversion Table
for Leaders & Tippet Diameters

Diameter (in)	Diameter (mm)	'X' Equivalent
0.020	0.50	
0.018	0.45	
0.016	0.40	
0.014	0.35	
0.012	0.30	
0.011	0.28	0X
0.010	0.25	1X
0.009	0.23	2X
0.008	0.20	3X
0.007	0.18	4X
0.006	0.15	5X
0.005	0.13	6X
0.004	0.10	7X
0.003	0.075	8X

Table of Fly Sizes
to Leader Tippets

Hook size	Tippet 'X' rating	Breaking strain (lb)	Breaking strain (kg)	Diameter (in)	Diameter (mm)
4–6	1X	9	4.08	0.010	0.25
6–8	2X	7	3.17	0.009	0.23
8–10	3X	6	2.72	0.008	0.20
8–14	4X	5	2.26	0.007	0.18
12–18	5X	4	1.18	0.006	0.15
12–20	6X	3	1.36	0.005	0.13
18–28	7X	2	0.90	0.004	0.10
18–28	8X	1	0.45	0.003	0.075

What Knots to Use

What Knots to Use

List of Knots & Rigs

Knots

Leaders and rigs

Knot Construction
—things to remember

1. Every precaution you take, from stalking the fish to wearing camouflage clothing will count for zip if the knot fails you because it isn't tied correctly.

2. Never, ever tighten down a knot without lubricating it first. This not only allows the knot to lock in correctly, but it decreases the amount of friction heat on the monofilament, which can decrease the breaking strain considerably.

3. Never jerk a knot tight, always tighten with a steady, and even pressure.

4. Hold the pressure on the knot for a couple of seconds after tightening. This allows the knot to lock into position correctly and not slip.

5. Always make sure that the knot is locked in correctly before trimming off the tag. On small flies leave a tag of ⅛ inch (3 mm) or so, and on larger flies it is possible to get away with a tag of ¼ inch (6 mm). Although this tag shouldn't be necessary, it never hurts to be cautious and allow for the possibility of knot slippage.

6. Where knots are tied that require doubling of the line, try to keep the lines parallel where possible rather than allowing them to twist. Incorrectly overlapping lines have a tendency to cut into the lower lines when tightening the knot.

Chapter 1

Knots

Fishing success and angling enjoyment come about more often than not when many little things are done correctly and without the angler being required to give them a second thought. One of the most important of these is the selection and tying of knots. If it isn't already a high priority, then I urge you to make it a priority to learn to tie a selection of knots, and for it to become second nature to select and tie the correct knot for the situation at hand.

Doubtless, we can all tie a proficient knot while sitting beside a calm pool in the middle of the day in lovely spring weather. Change that time of day to the evening with the last rays of daylight upon you. You're at the tail glide of a pool and the trout start sipping down no-see-ums. You suddenly realise that you still have on that size 12 Wulff that did all the damage to the trout population yesterday, and you know that you need to downsize to a size 24 in quick time if you're to save face over the evening drinks back at the lodge.

Yes, perhaps you should have been expecting the hatch to come off as it did-but let's assume you're new at this fly fishing caper and you weren't ready. Selecting those knots that suit your angling conditions, and practising them off-stream to the point where you can tie them without thinking, can give you that slight edge that could turn a slow day into a red letter one.

And just as with casting or fly tying, practice does at least make us proficient if not perfect, and with a couple of pieces of cord at the office and at home it doesn't take long to become adept at knot tying and for it to become second nature. I have included what I would consider the most commonly used knots in this book. Concentrate on practising those that are most applicable to your angling situations.

One thing that I would like to stress upon you that it is just as important as remembering the various knots and their tying. Whatever knot you select to use for whatever angling purpose, when using monofilament, always lubricate (with saliva) the knot before tightening down. Just as importantly, make sure that you stretch the knot and hold it for a few seconds at the time of tightening down so that when you release the pressure on the knot, it will stay locked permanently.

Arbor Knot (fresh and salt water)

This is a very fast and secure knot for attaching the backing to the fly reel. Pass the tag end of the backing line around the spool and form an overhand knot with the tag end around the main line. Then another overhand knot on the tag end of the line. Lubricate the knots if using monofilament, tighten down by pulling the main line, and trim the tag.

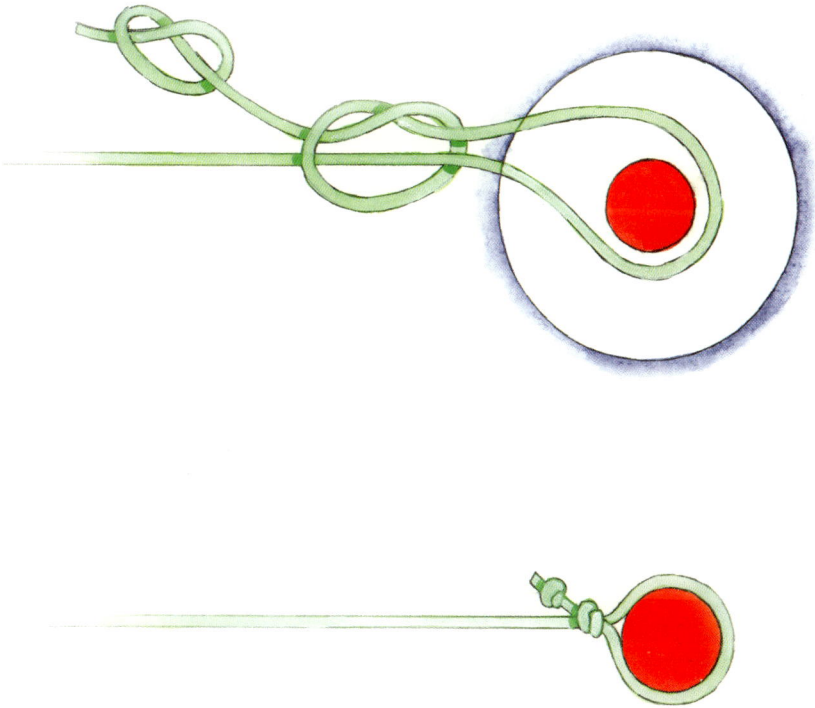

Nail Knot

This is a standard, permanent connection, leader to backing knot that is more commonly used for freshwater setups.

Double Nail Knot Loop

This knot is most often used at the leader end of the fly line. It is a less expensive knot than the Braided Loop but it is a far bulkier knot. It is useful for lighter saltwater fly fishing.

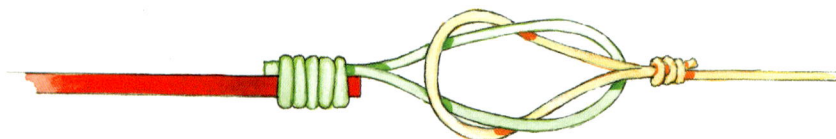

Braided Loop

This is the standard attachment for saltwater fly fishing where the angler is changing fly lines, as the fishing conditions demand, from floating to intermediates to shooting heads etc. The size of the loop at the back end of the fly line should be large enough to allow the fly reel to pass through for loop to loop connections. The loop at the head of the fly line needs to be only around 1 inch (2–3 cm) long. A braided loop connection is used in freshwater setups where the fishing conditions demand continual change of the complete leader.

Nail-less Nail Knot (fresh and salt water)

There are many tools on the market that help you to tie Nail Knots and, it seems, just as many versions of the Nail Knot itself. If you have bought the tools for these knots then you don't need retelling how to use them. I have included three tyings of the Nail Knot in this book and that should be more than necessary. My favourite is this one.

Hold here between thumb and forefinger

Flyline

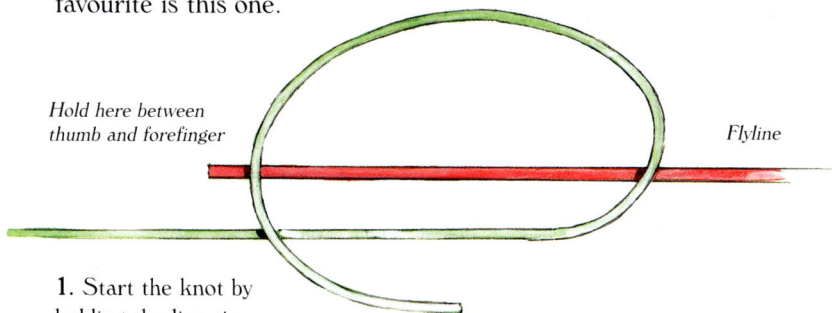

1. Start the knot by holding the line tip over the leader butt and forming a loop in the leader in front of the fly line. Pinch these lines between thumb and forefinger.

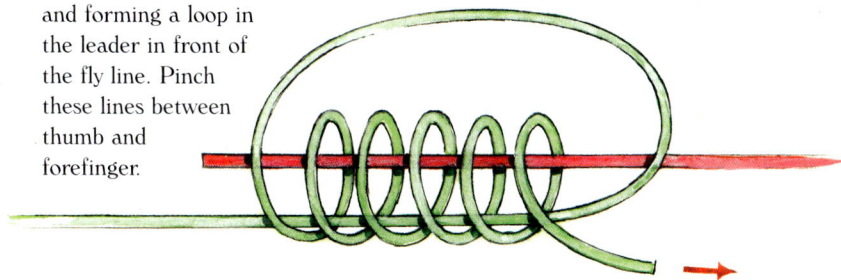

2. Pass the leader butt end through the loop and over the fly line six times, working the coils back towards the end of the fly line.

3. Pull the two leader ends slowly to tighten onto the fly line ensuring that the wraps of leader lay snugly against each other. Then tighten the knot by pulling the ends firmly. Trim the tag end of leader and fly line as close as possible to the knot.

Nail Knot (tube) (fresh and salt water)

This is the standard connection for attaching fly line to backing and leader. With near 100 percent in retained strength, this knot gets its name because it was originally tied using a nail. There are many tools available to help with tying this knot. I favour the Nail-Less Nail Knot—the less hardware you can get away with on the water the better as far as I'm concerned. However, the Nail Knot shown is relatively easy to master, and all you need is a piece of hollow tubing such as a piece of plastic that holds the ink in a ballpoint pen.

1. Place the fly line and tube parallel to each other, but coming in from the opposite direction, and lay approximately 8–10 inches (20–25 cm) of the butt end of the leader along the fly line also.

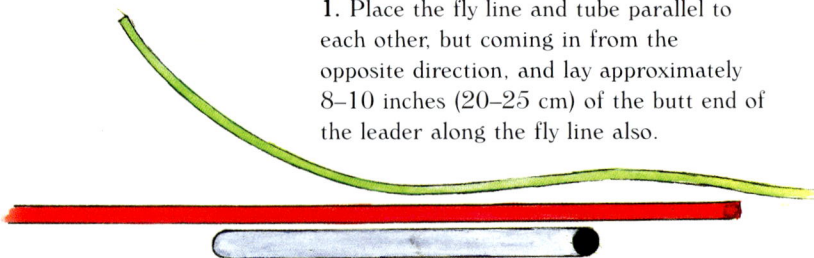

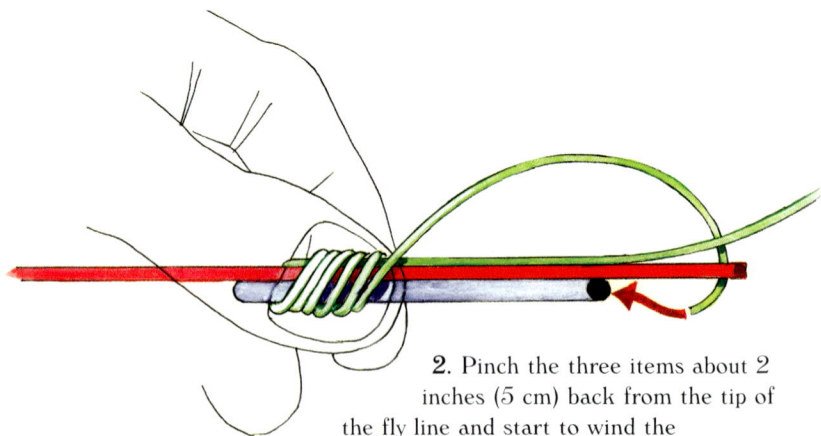

2. Pinch the three items about 2 inches (5 cm) back from the tip of the fly line and start to wind the monofilament back over itself, the fly line and the tube. Make five or six turns towards the end of the fly line, try to keep the wraps tight against each other. While still holding the turns tightly, pass the tag end of the leader through the hollow tube and pull this line until it loosely forms the knot shape.

3. Transfer the loose knot to the other hand and keep tightly pinching the knot. Pull the tube out from your grip of thumb and forefinger, away from the end of the fly line. At no time should you relax the pinching grip you have on the coils of the knot. Start to tighten knot by pulling on the tag end of the monofilament leader, you will feel when the knot has tightened to the point that you can release your grip.

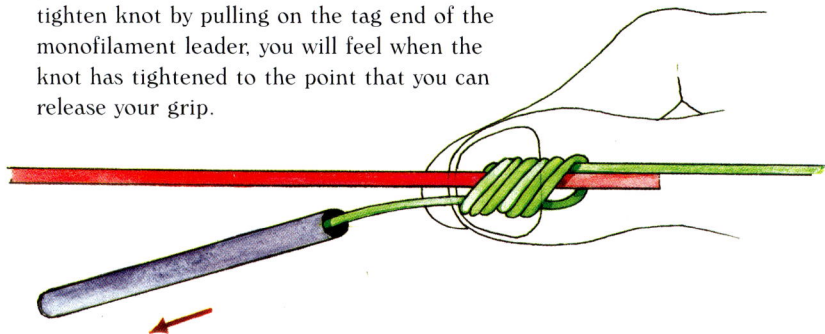

4. When you have released your pinching of the knot, you may notice that a few of the coils are not perfectly snug. Adjust these coils and then when satisfied that they are aligned, hold both the tag end of the monofilament and the leader end and pull as tightly as you can to lock down the knot. Trim the tag end of the monofilament and the fly line as closely as possible to the knot.

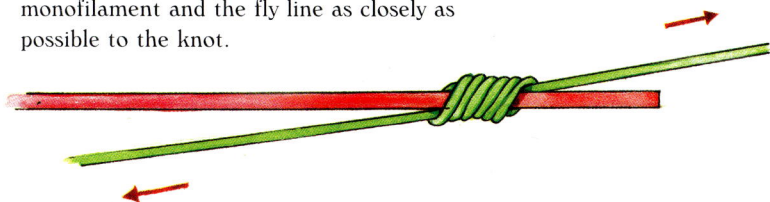

Double Nail Knot Loop (End Loop Knot) (fresh or salt water)

This knot is a standard Nail Knot tied with a doubled strand of monofilament.

1. Double the monofilament and hold it between thumb and forefinger along with tube and fly line. Wrap the doubled monofilament around the fly line and tube as with the traditional Nail Knot. Tuck the doubled tag ends of monofilament back through hollow tube. Change the hand that is holding the knot and remove the tube.

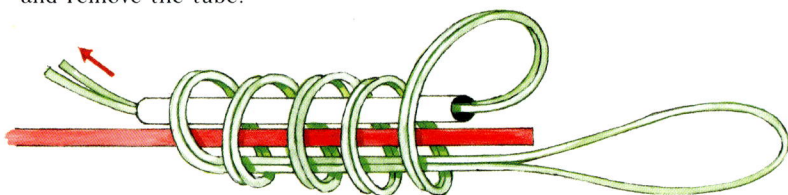

2. Tighten down the knot, making sure that the coils are snug and tight together. When tightened fully, trim the tag ends of monofilament and fly line and coat the knot with flexible glue.

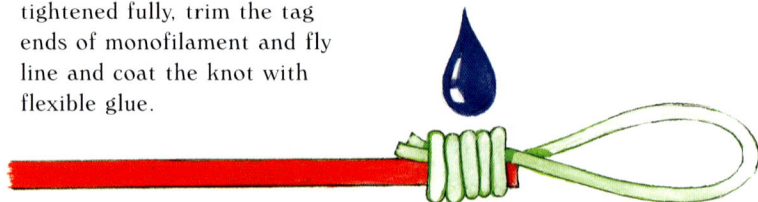

Constructing a Braided Loop

If you don't wish to buy commercially available Braided Loops then it is a simple process to construct your own. Cut a length of hollow braided line to the length you require, for a standard end of leader loop connection, 6–8 inches (15–20 cm) is adequate. You will also need a crochet hook, preferably one with a movable guard.

1. Start by threading the hook through the braid around 1 inch (2.5 cm) from the end and into the hollow section of the braid. Thread the hook inside the braid for about 2 inches (5 cm) and then back outside the braid. Pick up the braid with the hook end and pull the braid back through the centre of the braid and out the entry point. You can now adjust the size of the loop by pulling this threaded tag section.

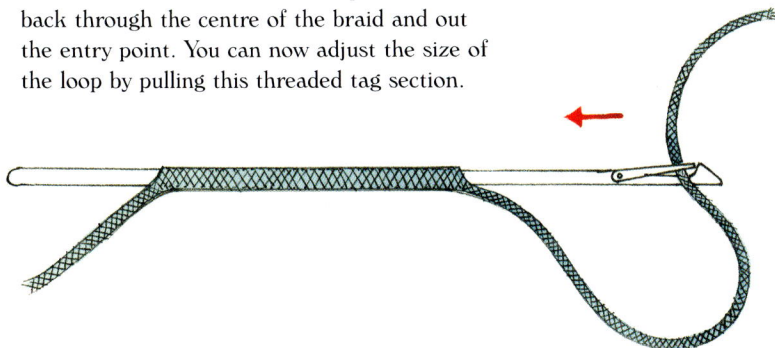

2. Trim off the single braid tag close to where it exits from the centre of the braid and trim the single braid just away from the doubled section. Add a drop of Superglue to where the loop starts.

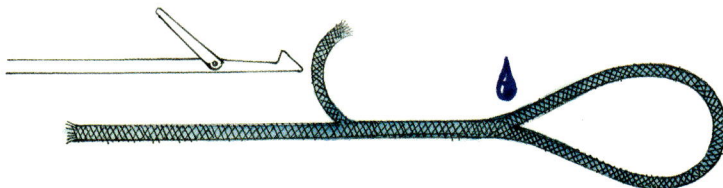

Braided Loop Attachment

Always trim the non-loop section of the Braided Loop to a maximum of 3 inches (8 cm) before attaching it to the fly line. This applies mostly to lighter fly lines, where the mass on the end of the fly line can effect the presentation of the fly. It does not apply to the same extent in saltwater fly lines however, 4–5 inches (10–12 cm) should be an adequate length to allow areas to whip and glue where the tubing is not required.

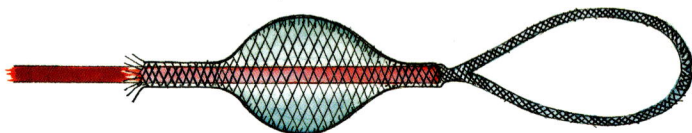

1. Slip the hollow end of the Braided Loop onto the end of the fly line and proceed to creep the loop along the fly line until the end of the fly line reaches the start of the loop. (Always ensure that you don't stop the fly line back from the loop, as it will create a hinge where the leader and loop meet. This hinge can prevent the leader from turning over correctly while casting.)

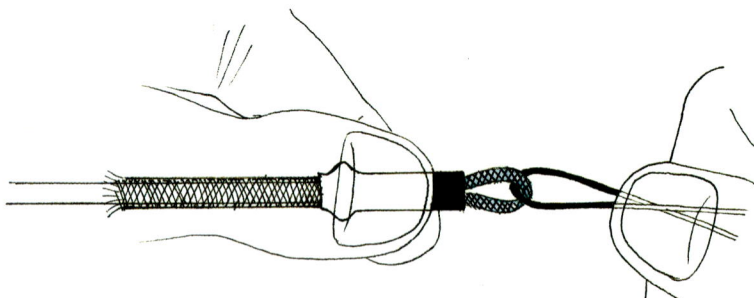

2. Hold the braid in place so that it doesn't creep back off the fly line. Loop a section of monofilament through the Braided Loop and thread a ¾ inch (2 cm) length of the flexible tubing over this loop of monofilament and then over the braid loop. Work the tube along the braid over the fly line until the tube is centred over the end of the braid and the fly line. Working this tubing along the braid-covered fly line takes some effort. The monofilament length through the braid loop gives you something to pull with against while working the tubing slowly along the braid.

3. The finished connection will not slip off while the tubing is in place. If you wish to remove the Braided Loop, simply roll tubing off the Braid and up the fly line and pull the Braided Loop slowly off the fly line.

When a permanent loop is required, especially when saltwater fly fishing, the tubing is dispensed with and the braid is held in place by whipping the braid onto the line in one or two places and coated with flexible glue.

Perfection Loop (fresh and salt water)

This is a very effective and reliable loop. It can take practice to get the tying right but once mastered, it makes a very neat and straight knot.

1. Start by forming a single loop behind the main line. Form a second, smaller loop in front of the first loop and then bring the tag behind the main line.

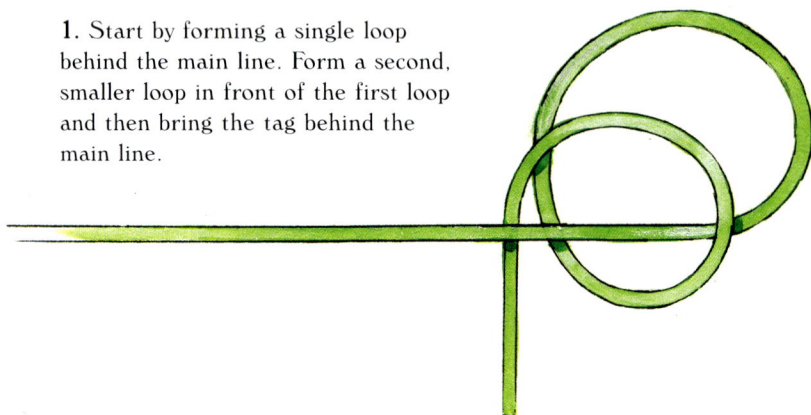

2. Hold the loops together between thumb and forefinger with the tag end coming out at right angles from the main line facing to the left. Now take the tag end and slip it between the two loops so that the tag is now protruding at right angles and is on the right of the main line and between the two loops. Pinch it between the same thumb and forefinger.

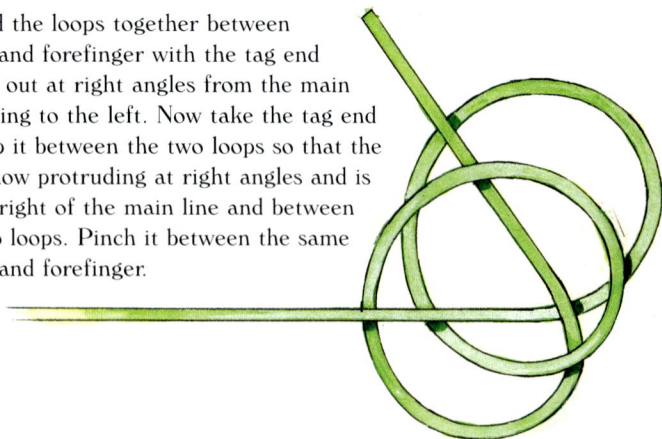

3. Reach through the first larger loop and pull the second smaller loop through it, making sure that the tag end of the knot stays in place on the right hand side. Start to tighten the knot by pulling on this second smaller loop away from the main line. Do not pull on the tag end of the knot.

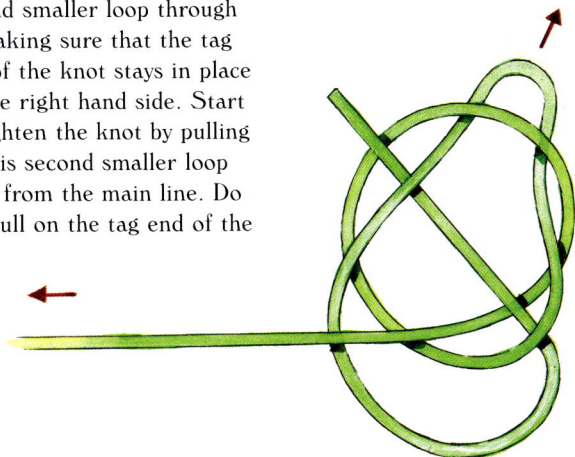

4. Lubricate the knot and tighten it completely. For the knot to be correctly tied, the tag end should be coming out from the knot at right angles to the main line. If this isn't the case then this knot needs to be removed and retied. Trim the tag when the knot is correctly aligned.

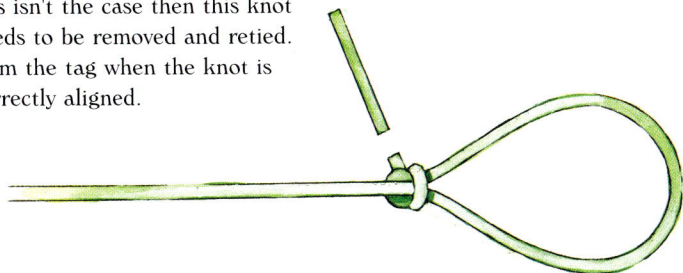

Double Grinner Knot (fresh and salt water)

The Double Grinner Knot is an alternative to the Blood Knot when wishing to join two pieces of line and using a dropper fly, where permitted. Cross over the two sections of the leader making sure to allow for the length of the dropper that you wish to fish, usually around 6–12 inches (15–30 cm). Hold the two pieces at the crossed section with your left thumb and forefinger, and with your right hand form a loop by returning the shorter section of leader back to the crossed section and grip it too with your left thumb and forefinger. Then pass the tip section back through the loop formed and around the other line four or five times. Tighten down this knot very lightly to hold it.

Proceed to do the other half of knot using the opposite hands. At the completion, lubricate the knot and pull both ends tightly so that both sides of the knot tighten and slide together. If it is your intention to use a dropper then just before you lock this knot down firmly, and before trimming off the tag ends of leader, take the longer tag end and pass it back through the loop formed between the two knots and the two leader sections. When the knot is pulled tight, this dropper section should stand out at right angles to the leader.

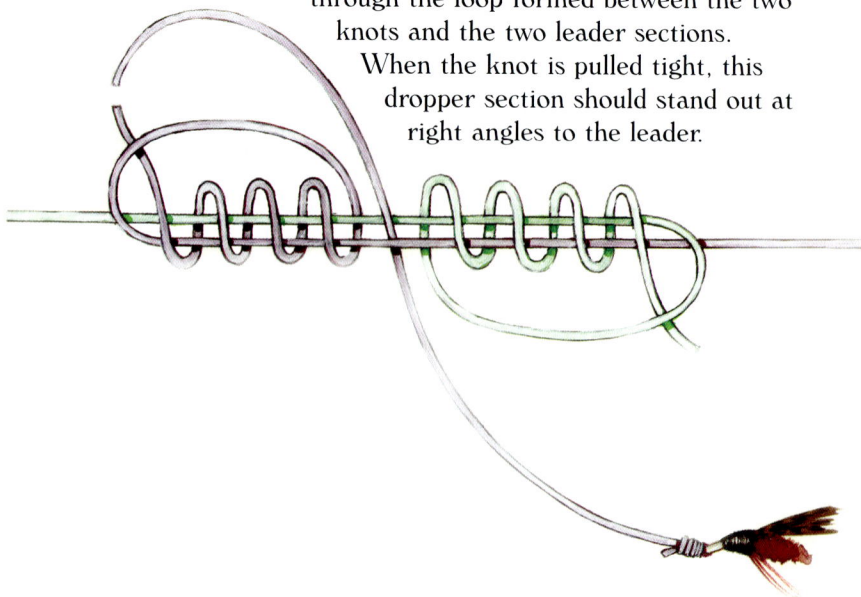

Blood Knot (fresh and salt water)

This is the most frequently used knot for joining two sections of like-diameter monofilament. Cross two 4 inch (5 cm) lengths of leader material over each other and hold the cross formed with your right thumb and forefinger. Use your left hand to make five turns with the short end of the leader around the long section twisting away from your thumb and forefinger. Bring back the short end and insert it through the other side of the crossed lines.

Now switch the knot over from your right to left thumb and forefinger, and repeat the process using the left tag end. Bring the tag back as before and thread it through the centre loop formed, but in the opposite direction to right hand tag.

Lubricate the loose knot with saliva and draw the knot tight before trimming the tag ends close to the knot.

This knot and the Double Grinner Knot make excellent dropper knots. When you start to tie this knot, simply allow one of the tag ends to be about 6–12 inches (15–30 cm) long. At the completion of the knot, trim the short tag end only, leaving the longer tag for the dropper.

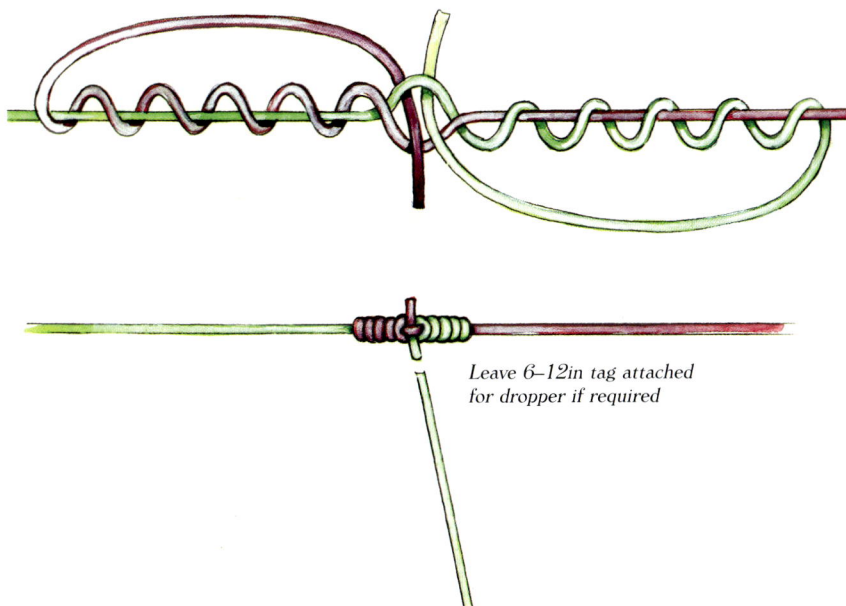

Leave 6–12in tag attached for dropper if required

Double Blood Knot (fresh water)

This is an alternative to the Double Surgeon's Knot for joining two sections of greatly varying diameter monofilament. The beauty of this knot is that it gives you a finished loop to which you can attach another section of looped monofilament for speedy use when a dropper of some type is necessary.

Tie it in the same way as the Blood Knot except that you double the thinner diameter tippet on itself before commencing to tie the knot. I have noted that this knot is only a freshwater knot. There are far better knots for joining varying diameter monofilaments, especially when dealing with heavier saltwater leader sections.

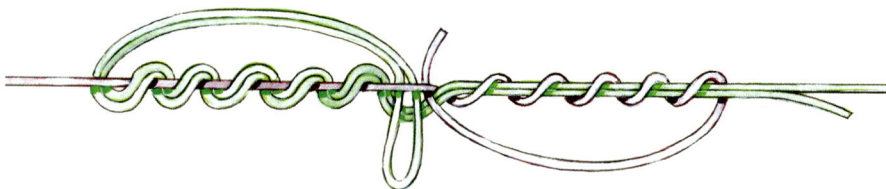

Surgeon's Loop (fresh and salt water)

This is a very simple knot that is extremely useful for attaching the tippet to the main leader. By using a loop to loop join as the last knot in the leader section, you will retain the main leader length at all times when the tippet section becomes too short and requires replacement.

Start the knot by taking the line back on itself to create a doubled length. Tie an overhand knot in the doubled line and then tuck the doubled end through the loop again. Lubricate the knot and pull it tight, try to keep the loop end to about ½ inch (1 cm) in length—longer for salt water. Trim off the tag end closely.

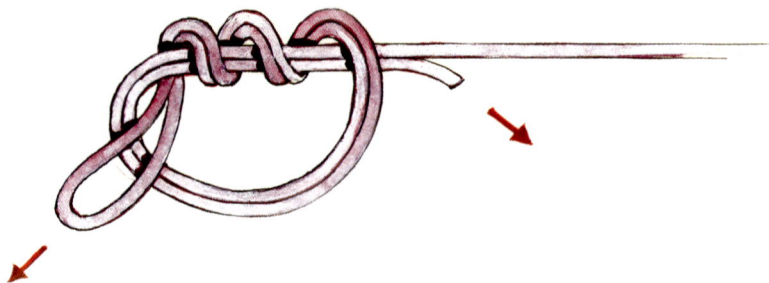

Double Surgeon's Knot (fresh and salt water)

This is the quickest knot for joining two sections of leader and is especially useful when the sections are very different in diameter.

Overlap two sections of leader by approximately 6 inches (15 cm). Form a 2 inch (5 cm) loop and tie in three overhand knots through the large loop. Lubricate the knot and pull steadily on all four ends to tighten. Trim the tag ends closely to the formed knot.

This knot is often used to form a dropper above a point fly. However, it is best only used when speed is of the essence, both the Double Grinner Knot and the Blood Knot make better droppers by allowing the droppers to stand at right angles to the main line.

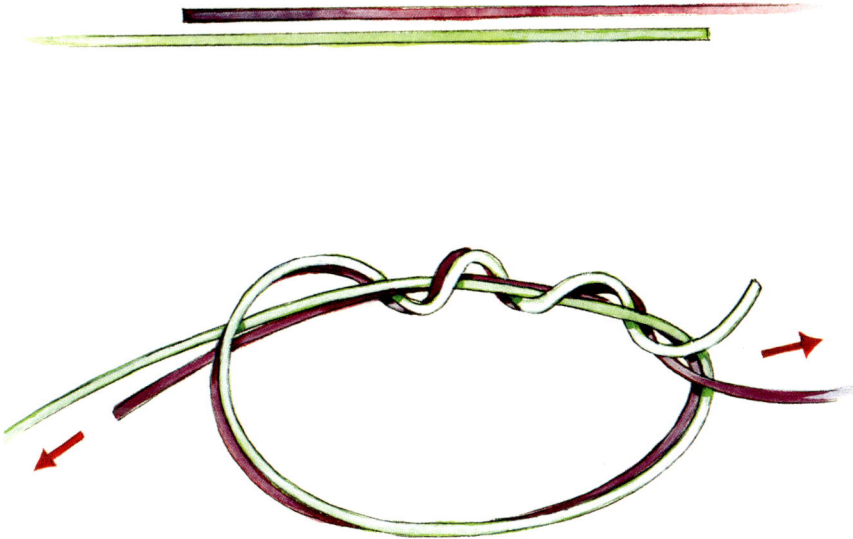

Interconnecting Loop to Loop
(fresh and salt water)

When using loop to loop connections for your leader to tippet sections, it is critical that the two loops sit correctly. This illustration shows the correct method. If these loops are not correctly joined then it is possible for the lines to cut into each other and destroy the integrity of the knot.

Connect the lines by sliding one loop over the other loop. Thread the tippet loop through the main leader loop and pull the connections tight so that the loops join.

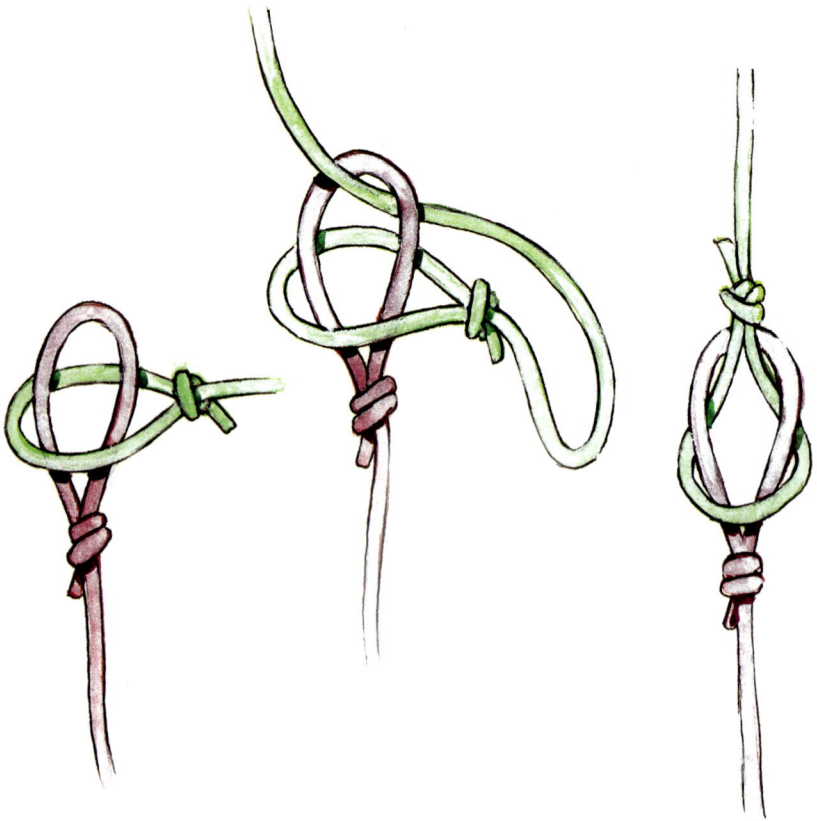

Double Line Loop (salt water)

This knot can be tied using monofilament or braid and is a simple double line loop knot where you may require extra line strength or especially in salt water where you may need to join a large diameter line to a thinner line.

1. Make a loop by overlapping the tag end of the line back onto the main line, bringing the tag end back by approximately 2 feet (60 cm). Make nine to ten wraps around the main line away from the loop end.

2. Now take the same number of loops back over the top of the previous wraps back towards the loop. On one arm of the main loop tie an overhand knot, lubricate the overhand knot and draw it tight.

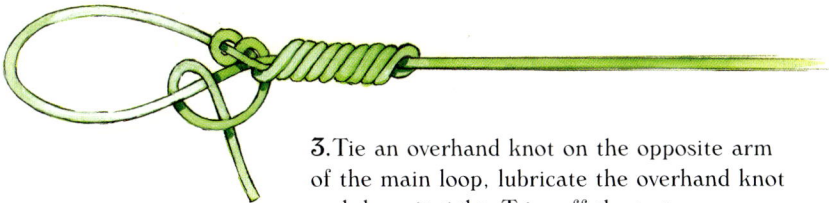

3. Tie an overhand knot on the opposite arm of the main loop, lubricate the overhand knot and draw it tight. Trim off the tag.

Spider Hitch (salt water)

This is an easy to tie and very effective double line loop that is predominantly used in salt water. It can also be tied using a pencil or twig etc. instead of your thumb and this method requires less line to tie. This knot is quick to tie, but is not as effective as the Bimini Twist Knot. It is another effective knot for attaching small diameter lines to large diameter lines.

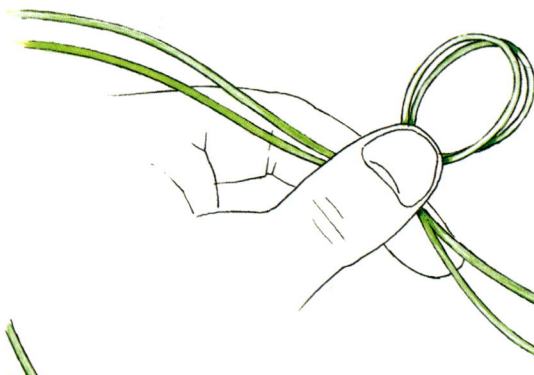

1. Form a large loop in the main line and form another, smaller loop by doubling over the already doubled lines between thumb and forefinger.

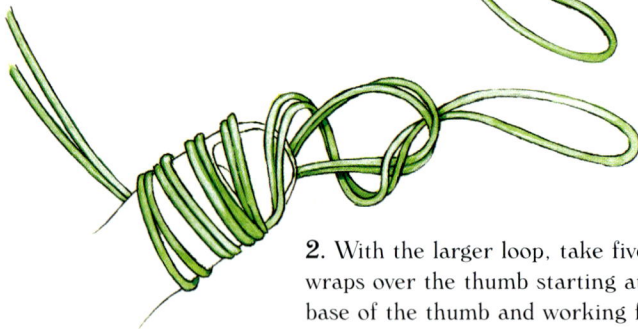

2. With the larger loop, take five or six wraps over the thumb starting at the base of the thumb and working forward. Pass the larger loop through the smaller loop at the end of the thumb and draw the loop through, pulling the coils off the thumb as you do so.

3. Lubricate the loose knot and tighten it by pulling on the main line and tag and the loop at the opposite end. Trim the tag.

Albright Knot (salt water)

The Albright Knot is a standard knot for saltwater fly fishing and is used when joining lines that are very different in diameter or when joining wire to monofilament.

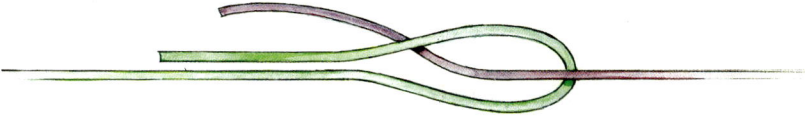

1. Form a loop in the tag end of the heavier line or wire making sure you allow 6 inches (15 cm) of overlap. Take the lighter line and pass the tag through the formed loop. Pinch both lines approximately 3 inches (8 cm) from the end, and at the same time allow approximately 3 inches (8 cm) of the lighter line to protrude beyond this point to tie the knot.

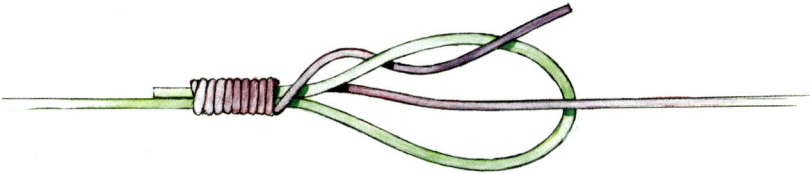

2. Start winding the lighter line back towards the end loop. Make at least ten tight turns of the lighter material back over the doubled section. Pass the lighter material through the end loop on the same side of the loop that the lighter line originally entered.

3. Very slowly, pull on the lighter line ends while grasping the heavier section and working the coils of the knot towards the loop end. Do not allow the coils to slip off the loop end. Keep working this knot until it is a snug fit at the end of the loop. Take special care when tying this knot as it is very prone to slipping if it is not tightened correctly.

Bimini Twist (salt water)

The Bimini Twist is used where you wish to retain 100 percent of the breaking strain of your line. It is used especially when fishing to IGFA rules and effectively acts as a shock absorber. It is used where you wish to join two lines and retain full line strength.

To effectively put a Bimini Twist in one end of a piece of monofilament and retain the single strand length required under the IGFA rules then you will need to start with a minimum of 6–8 feet (1.8–2.4 m) of line. If you require a knot in each end then you will need at least double this length of line.

1. Start the knot by doubling the line and place one hand through the loop. The other hand holds the tippet around the middle of the section. Put a minimum of twenty twists (the preferred number is 35 to 40) in the tippet by rotating your hand.

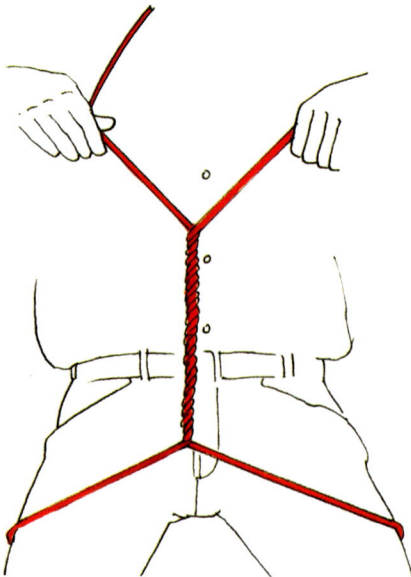

2. Take the loop and slip it over your knees to use as an anchor point for the loop and for you to apply upward pressure to the bottom of the coils in the line. Keep holding the middle section of line as you do so.

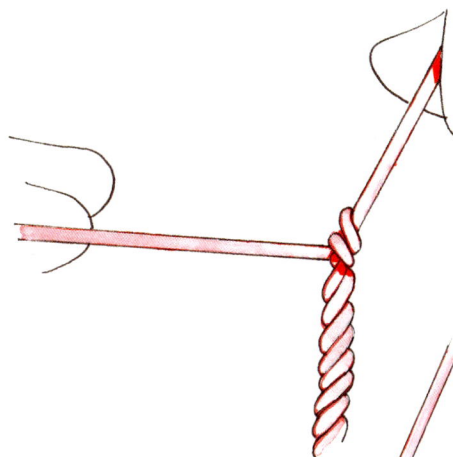

3. Hold the tag end of the monofilament with your free hand and with the twists forced tightly together and the standing line slightly off the vertical bring the tag end to a right angle from the twists.

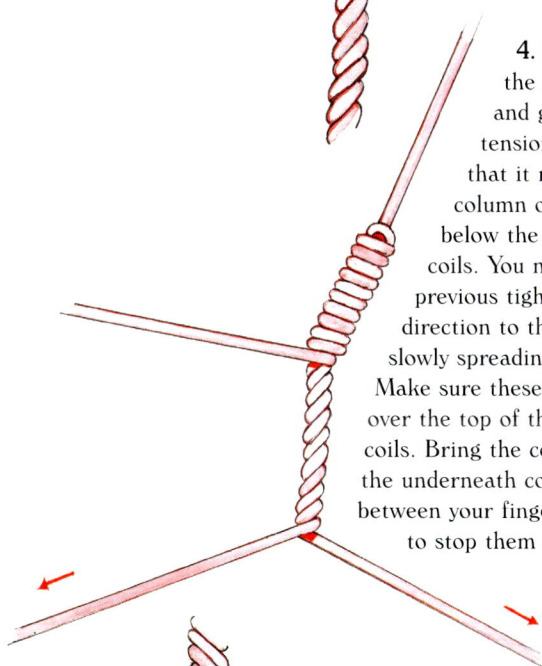

4. Keep the tension on the twists with your knees and gradually ease the tension off the tag end so that it rolls down over the first column of twists, starting just below the uppermost original coils. You now start to overlap the previous tight coils in the opposite direction to the original coils by slowly spreading your knees apart. Make sure these coils are snug and tight over the top of the original, underneath coils. Bring the coils along to the start of the underneath coils and pinch the coils between your fingers on main line hand to stop them from unravelling.

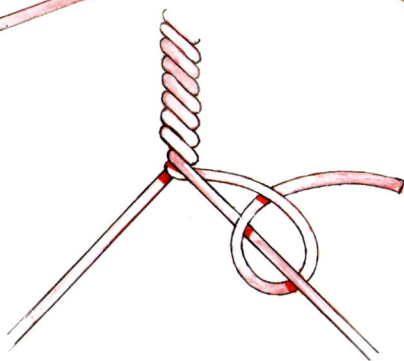

5. Take the tag end and tie an overhand knot in one of the loop arms, lubricate it and tighten it against the coils. The knot is now sufficiently secure to remove it from your knees without it unravelling, but keep the loop stretched out tight by hitching it over your foot.

6. Tie a half hitch around both arms of the loop, but do not tighten them.

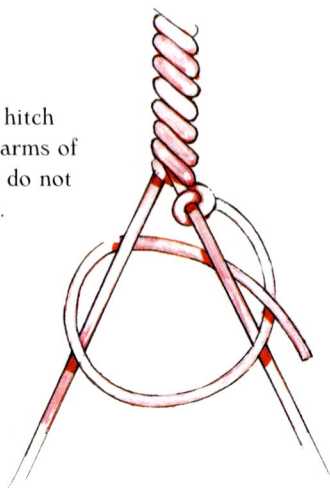

7. Make two more turns with the tag end around both legs of the loop, winding the tag inside the bend of line formed by the loose half hitch (tied in point 6) and back towards the main knot.

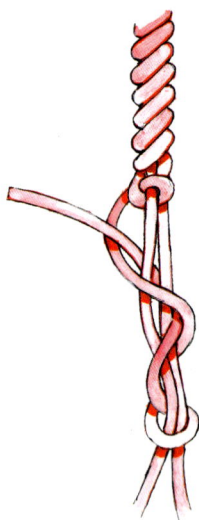

8. Lubricate this knot and start to tighten it by slowly pulling on the tag end of the line while working the knot down with your fingernail. Make sure that the knot is fully tightened before trimming the tag end.

Huffnagle Knot (salt water)

The Huffnagle is a very effective knot for attaching a very heavy, 80–120lb (35–60 kg) strain, monofilament shock tippet to a section of class tippet that has been doubled with a Bimini Twist.

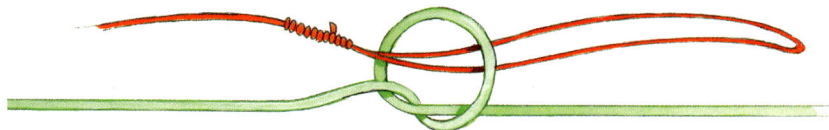

1. Make an overhand knot in the shock tippet leaving about 4 inches (10 cm) of the tag end. Pass the Bimini Twist loop through the overhand knot and lubricate the overhand knot.

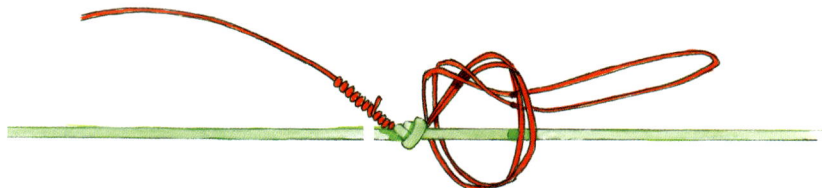

2. Tighten the overhand knot and pull it along the loop line up to the Bimini Twist knot. Trim the tag end of the shock tippet and then tie an overhand knot in the Bimini Twist loop (class tippet) around the shock tippet, lubricate it and tighten. Take the loop again and form another overhand knot, lubricate it and tighten.

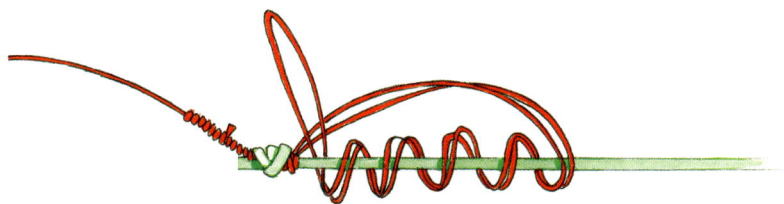

3. Take the tag end of the loop and make five wraps over the shock tippet back towards the figure eight knots.

4. Lubricate the knot and begin to tighten it by pulling on the tag end, working the coils back towards the central knot. Fully tighten the knot and trim the tag.

Clinch Knot (fresh water)

The Clinch knot and the Improved Clinch Knot are the two most commonly used knots for attaching the fly to the leader in freshwater fly fishing.

The Clinch Knot can also be used for attaching dropper sections to the main leader above a leader join knot or to a dropper loop in the main leader such as a Double Blood Knot or a Slip Knot.

Thread the leader through the hook eye and wrap the end back up the leader five times. Thread the leader back through the first loop in front of the hook eye. Lubricate the knot and pull steadily to tighten it against the hook eye. When tightening, hold the tag end of the tippet against the fly to avoid knot slippage. Trim the tag end.

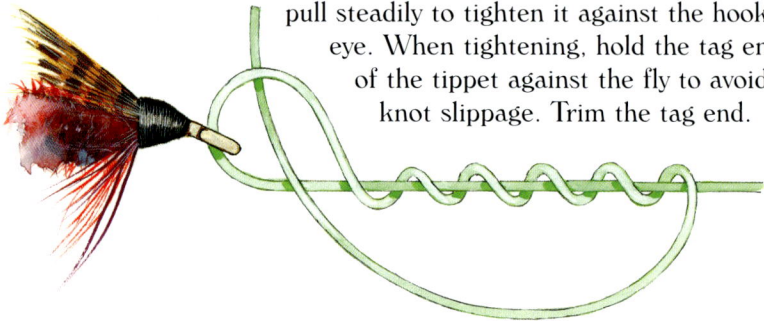

Improved Clinch Knot (fresh water)

This is the most common knot for attaching the fly to the leader. Thread the leader through the hook eye and wrap the end back up the leader five times. Thread the end of the leader back through the first loop in front of the hook eye and then back through the large loop just formed. Wet the knot and pull steadily on the tippet to tighten the knot against the eye of the hook. Trim the tag of line after the knot is tightened leaving a small tag for slippage.

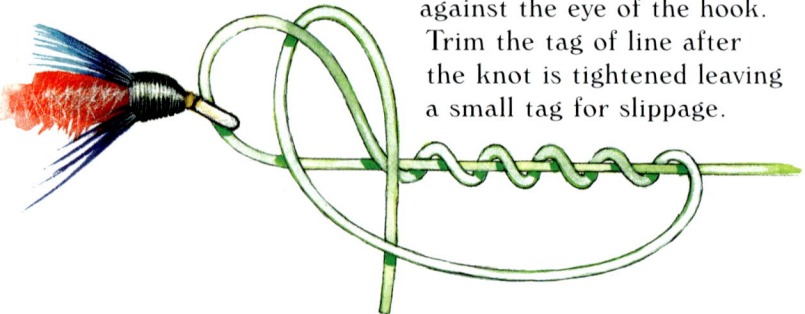

Grinner Knot (fresh and salt water)

This knot is tied exactly the same as the Duncan Loop with the exception that instead of leaving a loop at the hook eye as in the Duncan; with the Grinner you need to draw the finished knot down to the hook eye. It is a very strong knot, however it does use up more of your precious tippet material than the equally effective Improved Clinch Knot.

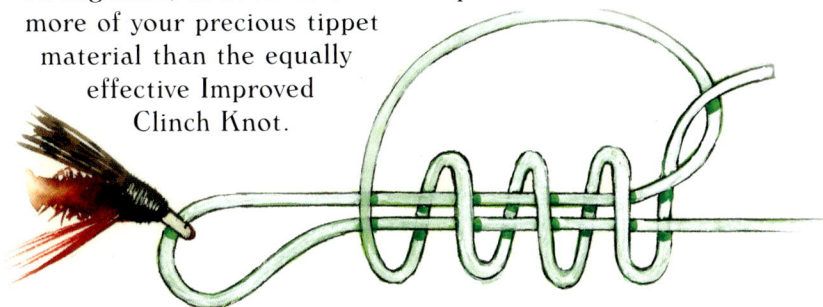

Trilene Knot (fresh and salt water)

This is an excellent knot for joining leader to fly, for both fresh and salt water. It is slightly bulkier than the Clinch Knot and therefore is more commonly used for attaching larger flies.

Thread the leader through the hook eye twice and wrap it back up the leader five times. Thread the leader back through the two loops formed at the hook eye. Lubricate the knot and pull steadily to tighten the knot against the eye of the hook. When tightening, hold the tag end of the tippet against the fly to avoid knot slippage. Trim the tag end of the tippet.

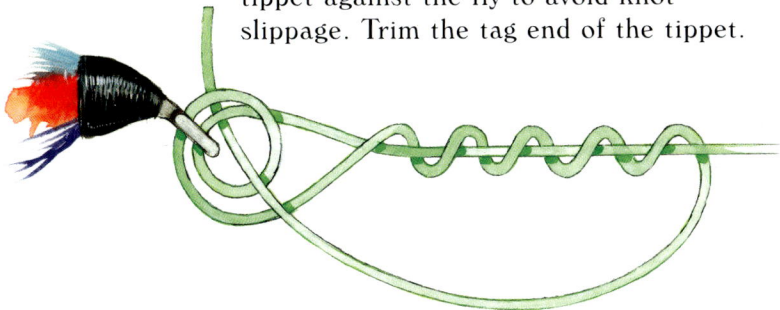

Figure Eight Turle Knot (fresh water)

Turle knots are, to some extent, outmoded in fly fishing circles of today. They are for use on up-eye hooks generally-both trout and salmon. They do give a straight connection to the fly and don't allow any hinging where the tippet joins the hook. Mainly out of interest, I have included two examples of the Turle Knot and illustrated their tying.

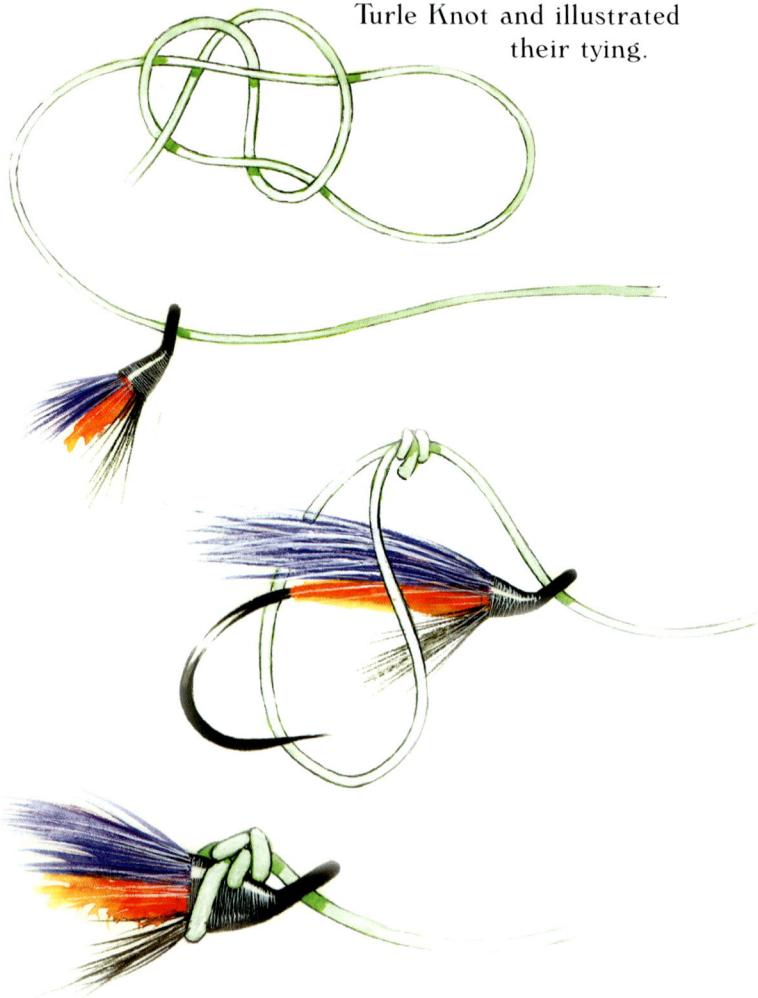

Double Turle Knot (fresh water)

The same comments as for the Figure Eight Turle Knot apply to this knot.

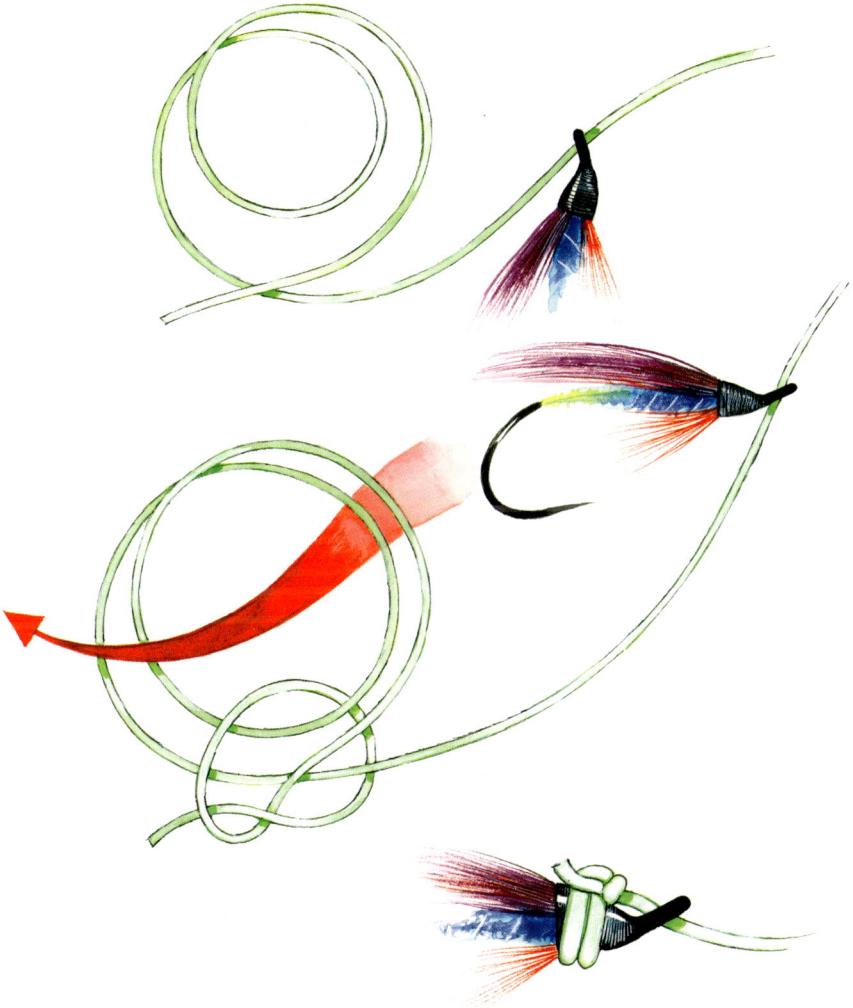

Riffle Hitch (fresh water)

The Riffle hitch is simply a hitch taken over the head of the fly after the initial knot, such as a Clinch Knot etc., has been tied. The hitch is tightened down so that the leader will come away from the eye of the fly on the right or left of the fly, or in the case of a double salmon fly hook, the leader should come away from under the throat of the fly. Although a knot used predominantly by salmon fishers, it can be deadly when fishing a skittering caddis fly across the surface, creating a fish-exciting skating effect. When used on large dry flies after dark, this hitch can help create a lot of fish-attracting surface disturbance with a slow fly retrieval.

Palomar Knot (fresh and salt water)

At virtually 100 percent line strength, this knot is easy and quick to tie, the Palomar is a knot well worth learning. Because it uses line that is doubled over in the tying it is more suitable for use on medium to large flies.

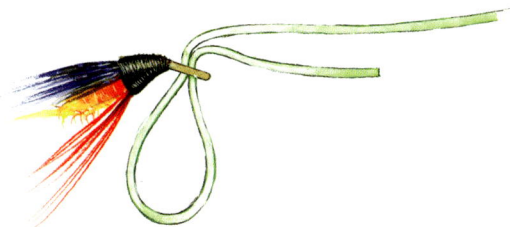

1 and 2. Form a loop approximately 9 inches (23 cm) long. Pass the loop through the hook eye and tie an overhand knot using the loop and the main line. Do not tighten this knot.

3. Take the loop end and pass the fly through this loop.

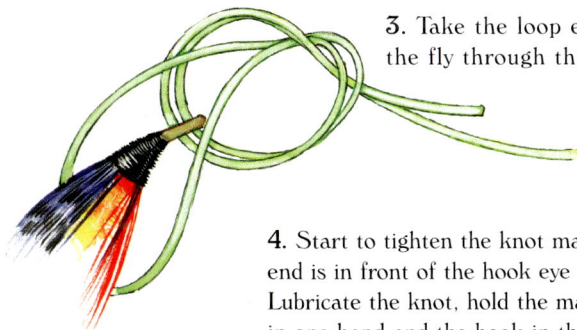

4. Start to tighten the knot making sure that loop end is in front of the hook eye when drawn tight. Lubricate the knot, hold the main line and tag end in one hand and the hook in the other, and draw the knot tight. Trim the tag.

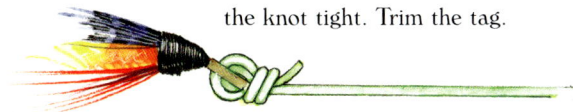

Duncan Loop (salt water)

This is a popular knot for saltwater fly fishing as it allows the fly to swing freely at the end of the leader.

Thread the tippet through the hook eye and pull back around 6 inches (15 cm) of tippet parallel to the main line. Form a loop by bringing the tag end back towards the hook eye and make five turns back around the doubled line.

Pull the tag end slowly until the knot begins to form. Slide the knot to the desired size and lubricate it. Tighten the knot fully by pulling on the tag end of the leader and the hook end with pliers.

Trim the tag.

Often when you hook a fish and weight is applied, the knot will slide closed against the hook eye. Once the fish has been landed, simply slide the knot back to reform the loop.

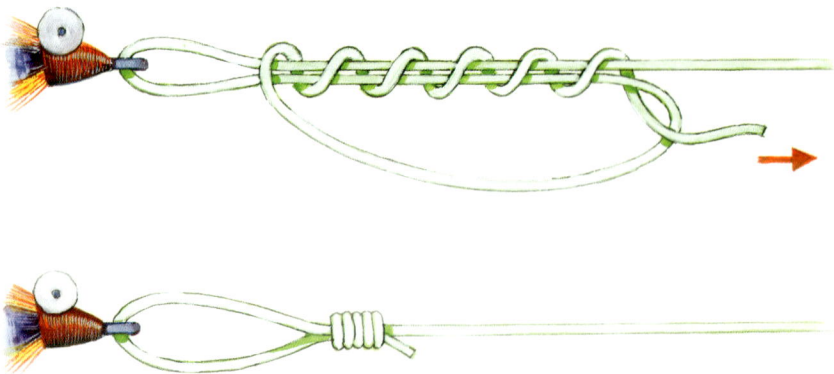

Homer Rhode Knot (salt water)

This knot should never be used on lighter weight monofilaments. It breaks at around 50 percent of the line test, so it is more suitable for heavier shock tippets, well above the class tippet weight.

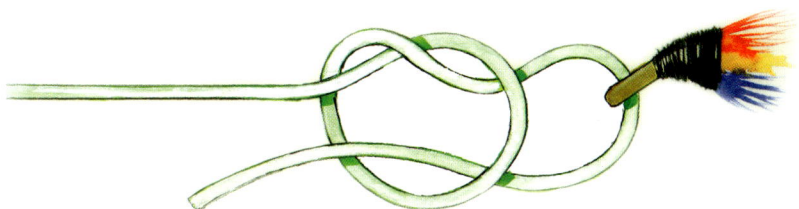

1. Form an overhand knot in the main line leaving approximately 8 inches (20 cm) of monofilament between the knot and the tag end. Pass the tag end through the hook eye and then back through the overhand knot from the same side as it exited.

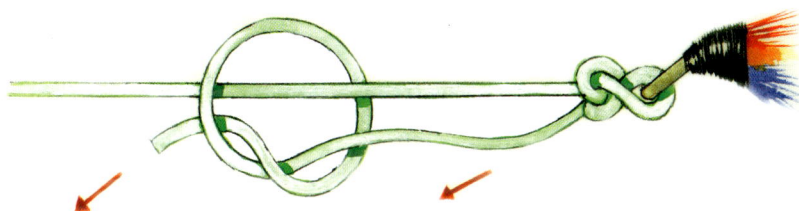

2. Tighten the overhand knot lightly to the hook eye by pulling on the tail of the fly and on the tag end of the line while keeping the two lines parallel to prevent the fly from twisting on the knot. Make another overhand knot over the standing part of the tippet. This knot is the stopper for the loop, so its position determines the size of the loop, generally this knot would be 1 inch (2–3 cm) from the hook eye.

3. Tighten this second knot and then pull on the bend of the fly hook and the main line at the same time. The knot at the hook eye should slide up the line snugly into the second knot. Trim the tag.

No-Slip Monofilament Loop (salt water)

As the name suggests, this loop knot won't slip tight under pressure as the Duncan Loop does. It is predominantly a knot for saltwater use and it rates at almost 100 percent line strength.

1. Start with approximately 12 inches (30 cm) of the tag end of the tippet and form an overhand knot, but do not tighten this knot.

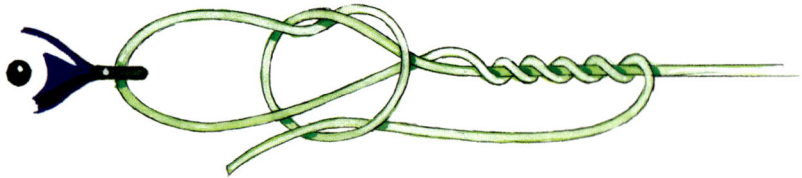

2. Now pass the tippet end through the hook eye and back through the overhand loop on the same side as the tippet exited the overhand loop. At this stage, decide on the size of the loop that you require and this is gauged by the distance between the hook eye and the overhand knot. With the tag end of the tippet make six turns around the main line and bring the tag back over and through the overhand knot. Make sure that the tag goes back through the overhand loop the same way that it was threaded originally.

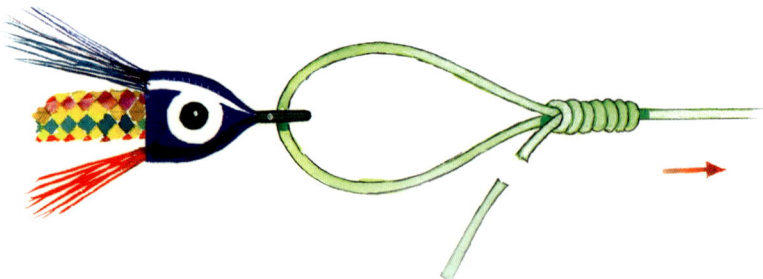

3. Lubricate the knot and it tighten by pulling on the tag end until the knot comes down onto the overhand knot, then pull on the fly and the main line to fully tighten the knot. Trim the tag.

Haywire Twist (salt water)

The Haywire Twist is used for attaching single strand wire to your fly on one end and a loop on the other end for attaching the tippet.

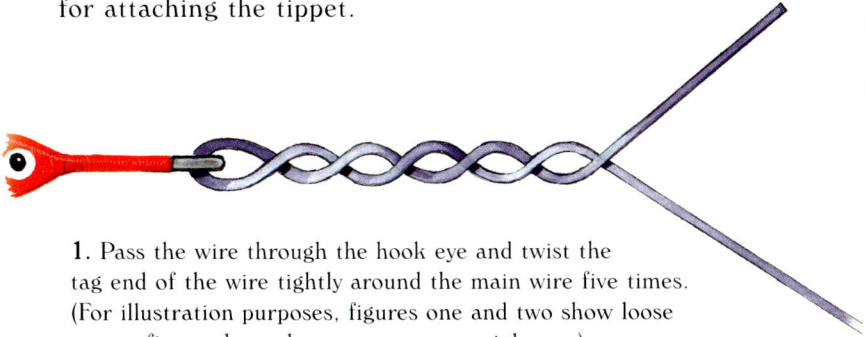

1. Pass the wire through the hook eye and twist the tag end of the wire tightly around the main wire five times. (For illustration purposes, figures one and two show loose wraps, figure three shows correct wrap tightness).

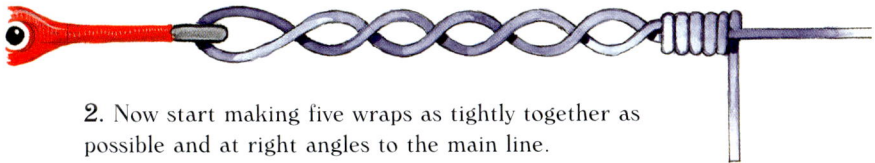

2. Now start making five wraps as tightly together as possible and at right angles to the main line.

3. The final part of the Haywire requires a handle to be formed in the remaining tag end. This handle is then used to twist around until the tag snaps off. Never use pliers to trim this tag end as it can create a very sharp and dangerous point.

Chapter 2

—— Strike Indicator Knots ——

There are numerous commercial strike indicators on the market, each seems to have its own pros and cons.

Here are two very simple knots that are perfectly adequate, simple to tie and work well with yarn indicators.

Duncan Loop Indicator Knot (fresh water)

The diagram explains the construction of this knot. Use a lightweight section of monofilament for this knot and tie it wherever required along the leader.

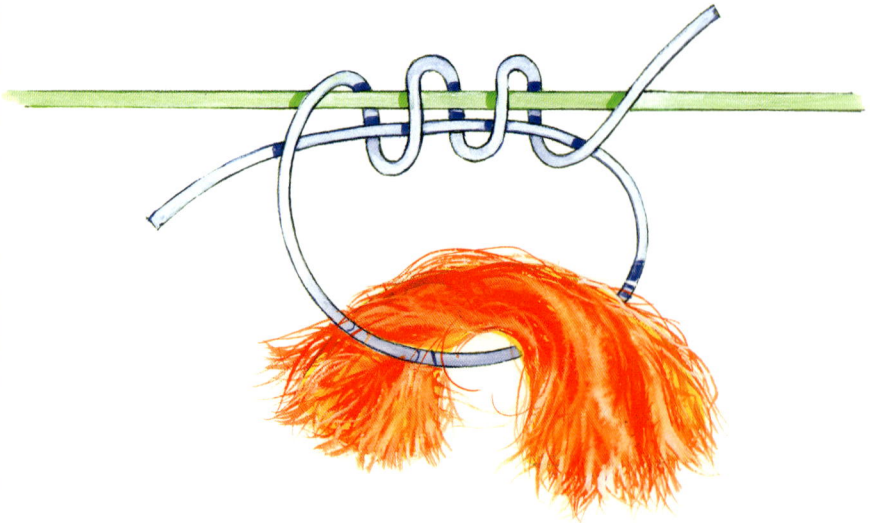

Slip Knot Indicator Knot (fresh water)

Tie a simple overhand knot as illustrated at any point along
the leader length. Insert the indicator yarn of your choice
and draw the knot closed.

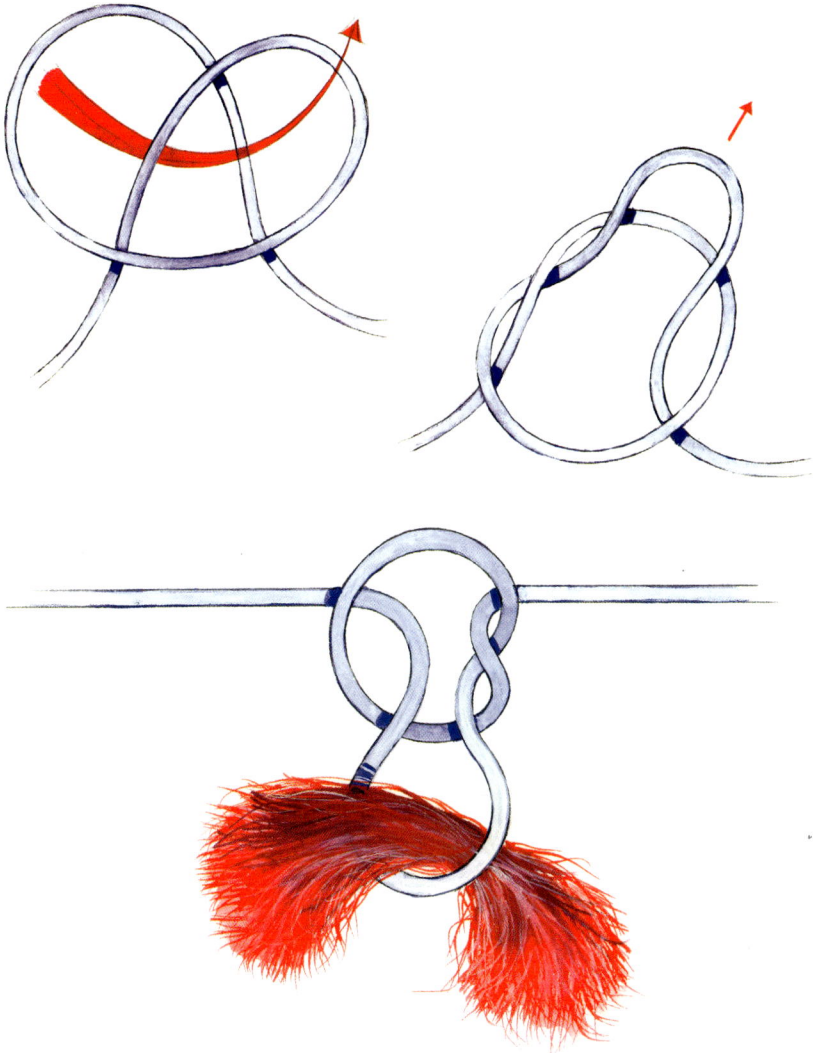

Chapter 3

— Tandem Fly & Dropper Rigs —

Dropper Rigs

Droppers and trailing flies can be very efficient ways of searching the water and there are many combinations of dropper and trailing fly rigs. One word of caution before rigging up with multiple or weighted flies, or even placing shot or weight to your leader-there are countries, regions and specific waters that have regulations that limit certain fly fishing methods. Always make it your business to be aware of the fishing regulations in the area that you intend to fish.

Leader Dropper Rig

The most common use of leader dropper rigs is on the British 'Loch style' fishing. Generally, a team of three flies is used with two of them on droppers and then the point fly. The dropper length is usually no longer than 6–10 inches (15–25 cm), any longer than this and the rig can become tangled. However, there are several other arrangements where dropper rigs are effective. A Surgeon's Knot is sometimes recommended for the dropper knot and when speed in rigging is a priority, this knot is adequate. My choice however is for the use of the Double Grinner or Blood

1

Large Wetfly with Nymph Dropper

1. A large wet fly on the point with a traditional wet fly or smaller nymph dropper.

2

Team of Wets

2. A team of traditional winged wet flies or nymphs, usually with a slightly larger wet on the point.

3

Loch style (two droppers and point fly)

3. Loch style, often two palmered flies on droppers with a winged wet fly on point.

4

Wetfly with Weighted Dropper

4. A wet fly on point with a dropper off the main leader. Where permitted, a split shot of weight can be attached to this dropper and, if required, a strike indicator can be attached along the leader.

5

Nymph with Strke Indicator

Strike indicator

5. A standard, single nymph with adjustable strike indicator.

Knot, both of these knots bring the tag out at right angles to the main line, thereby reducing tangles and allowing the fly to fish freely. The Surgeon's Knot trails the fly parallel to, and in contact with, the main line, increasing the chances of tangling and fouling the main leader. The question of when to use monofilament or fluorocarbon is an individual choice. I tend to use fluorocarbon only when I am going to be bouncing flies along the bottom of the stream. Do not be afraid to use monofilament and fluorocarbon together in a leader setup, they are perfectly compatible.

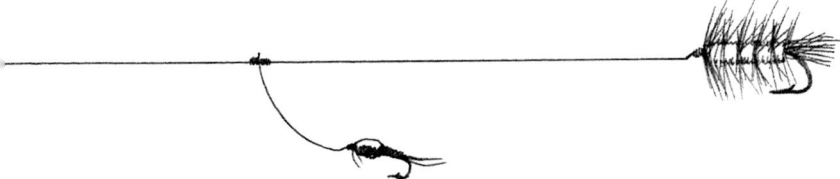

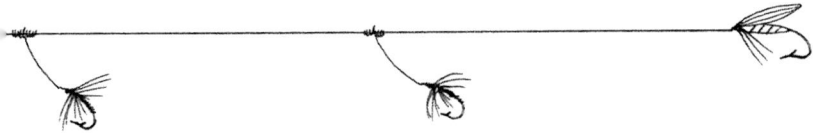

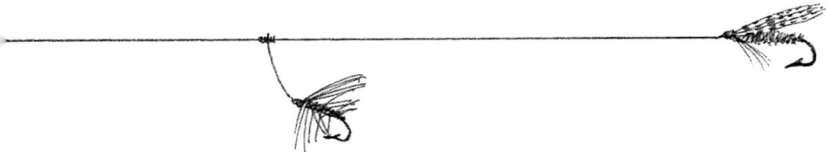

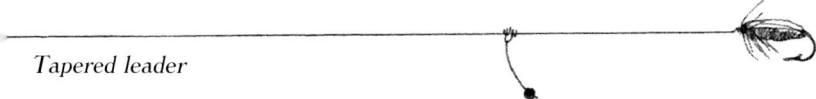

Tapered leader

Split shot

Tapered leader

Bend of hook dropper rig

This is the standard rig setup where the dropper is attached to the hook bend of the preceding fly. Any number of fly combinations can be used with this setup. At times dropper leaders are attached to the eye of the dry fly, I don't recommend

6 *Tapered leader*

Two nymphs (or wets) bend of hook dropper

6. It is often worthwhile using a nymph tied with a tungsten bead on the leader and a smaller unweighted nymph as the tail fly. If the water is deep and fast and you want to get the flies down to the bottom quickly without using large heavy flies, then place two tungsten nymphs one after the other with a short dropper, and the smaller unweighted nymph on the point.

7 *Tapered leader*

Two dry fly bend of hook dropper

7. This is a setup that is often used when you are in doubt as to what fly the fish are feeding on, or when the fish are feeding on very small insects and the angler is having trouble keeping visual track of the fly on the water. The larger fly allows the angler to keep in visual contact with the flies, even in low light conditions.

8

Dry fly with nymph dropper

8. This is the standard freestone river searching rig. When I'm in doubt as to whether the fish are up and feeding on the surface, this is the first rig I use. The dropper length on this rig should match the depth of water being fished.

this setup when this rig is used to fish both the stream surface and the stream bed at the same time, as the dry fly does not float correctly. If the dry fly is being used just as an indicator, then a strike indicator is the better and more effective option.

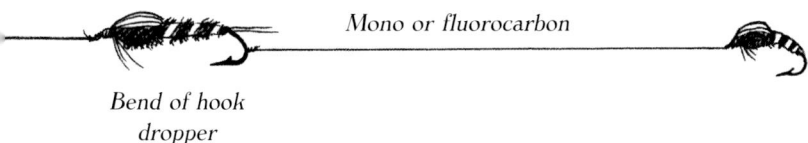

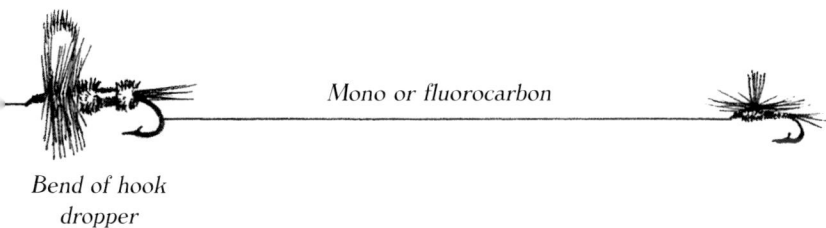

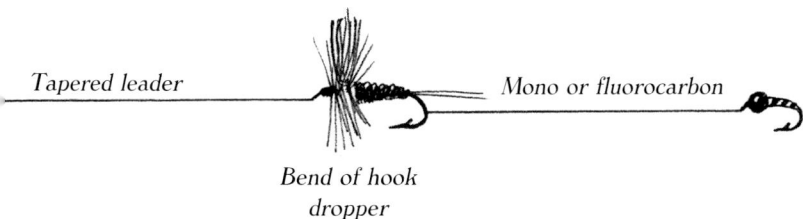

Mono or fluorocarbon

Bend of hook
dropper

Mono or fluorocarbon

Bend of hook
dropper

Tapered leader

Mono or fluorocarbon

Bend of hook
dropper

Chapter 4

—————— Leader Types ——————

There are five basic leader types that are available on the market and, within these five types, there are many combinations and variations. The five types are:

Commercial Tapered Leader (Knotless)

1

1. Knotless tapered leader

These can be used as standalone leaders or adjusted to suit your particular requirements. They come in various lengths and tippet breaking strains. A big disadvantage of these

Commercial or Hand-tied Leader (Knotted)

2

2. Knotted tapered leader

These are available commercially in various lengths and tippet breaking strains. In the chapter 'Leader Recipes' all of the tapered leaders are tied for specific fishing situations. If you are a regular fly angler then at some stage you will no doubt start tying your own leaders. A large section of this book is based around the knots that you can use to build your own leaders and rigs.

Commercial Tapered Poly Leader

3

3. Tapered Poly Leader

These are available in various lengths, tapers and weights. Simply loop on a length of tippet section to a Poly Leader and start fishing. Poly Leaders are a monofilament-type core with an outer flexible polyethylene coating. Generally they are far greater in diameter at the butt than Knotless

——➤ Knotless

leaders is that if you don't add an extra tippet section to them,
eventually the leader becomes too short and heavy after just a few fly
changes. Knotless leaders come into their own when used as the tapered
section of a personalised leader.

——➤ Knotted

——— Poly

Monofilament tippet section

Leaders and it is therefore possible to add tippets up to 10 feet (3 m)
in length to the poly section and still get a good turnover of leader
when casting. However, the drawback of this larger diameter butt can
be a decrease in leader presentation delicacy at the butt section of the
leader.

Leader Types

Tapered Braid Leader

4

4. Tapered Braided Leader

These are similar to the Poly Leaders in that what you are
buying is really only the heavy butt and tapered section of the
leader. Once purchased it is then up to the angler to attach
the tippet section and this section can be very long, allowing
for very delicate fly presentations. There are two main
disadvantages of the braided leader. The first is that the

Combination Commercial and Hand-tied Butt and Tippet sections

5

Heavy butt mono

*Commercial tapered leader
(trimmed off tippet section)*

5. Combination Tapered leader

This is my choice when it comes to leader selection, although I
admit that a certain amount of this preference is due to
laziness on my part when it comes to tying up full knotted
leaders. As with everything in this book, I have given you many
variations so that you can determine your own preference. I
have found that most, if not all Knotless Leaders have too thin
a butt section for my liking, so I just trim off the butt loop and

Monofilament tippet section

leader retains water and therefore when lifting the leader from the water when casting, it is possible to get a shower of spray back across the water when performing a false cast. The second and bigger disadvantage that I find with braided leaders is that after fishing for a while they tend to accumulate fine sand, dirt and slime within the braid and this considerably reduces the braid's floating ability.

New tippet section added to suit

join a heavier section, generally 1–2 feet (30–60 cm), of monofilament to this end. Knotless Tapered Leaders also have a front section of straight monofilament that starts at around 2–3 feet (60–90 cm) from the tip. Cut this section off and add a new section or sections to suit your angling situation. If you tie a loop knot at the end of the tapered section, it is possible to adjust the tippet section to suit the angling as many times as you like without reducing the length of the main leader.

Chapter 5

—————— Leader Recipes ——————

Leader design is based around the type of fishing that
you intend to do, the size and weight of the flies and rod
you will be using and the waters you fish. Once the above
have been determined, it is possible to personalise
leaders to specifically suit your fishing. I have included a
number of formulas for various water types and fishing
situations.

Leaders can be broken down into three sections.

1. The heavy butt section, which attaches to the fly line.
2. The centre or tapered section, which breaks the leader
down in sections from heavy at butt to lighter at tip. This
helps when transferring energy down the leader from butt to
tippet.
3. The tippet or presentation section of the leader. In some
instances such as when fishing for IGFA records or chasing
fish that have sharp teeth or gill rakers, another section
called the shock tippet can also be added to the three
sections above. This is usually made from heavy stiff
monofilament or wire.

It is worth mentioning that you should always try and fish a
leader that is the shortest, strongest and has the fewest
number of knots possible at all times. This equates to
efficient fishing, and that should always be your aim.

Small Stream Leaders

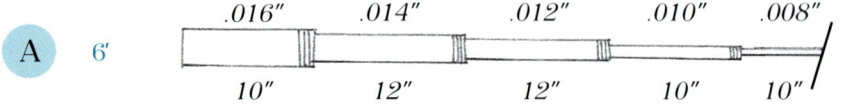

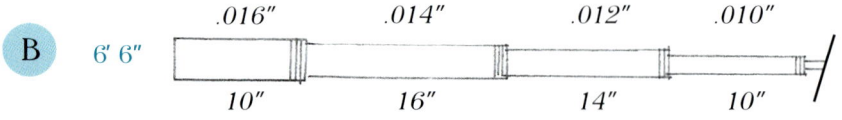

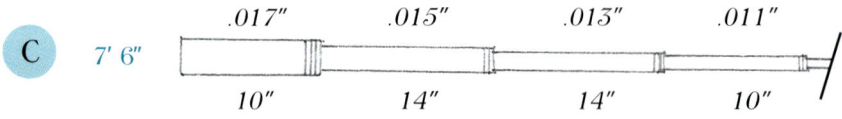

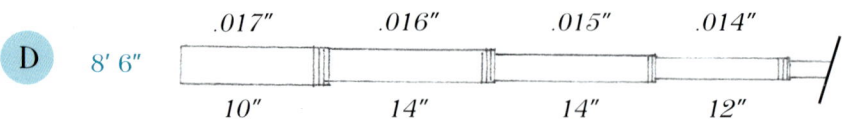

A   6'

.016"   .014"   .012"   .010"   .008"

10"   12"   12"   10"   10"

B   6' 6"

.016"   .014"   .012"   .010"

10"   16"   14"   10"

C   7' 6"

.017"   .015"   .013"   .011"

10"   14"   14"   10"

D   8' 6"

.017"   .016"   .015"   .014"

10"   14"   14"   12"

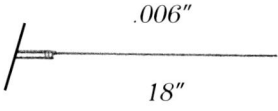

.006″

18″

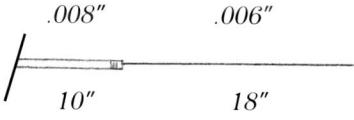

.008″   .006″

10″   18″

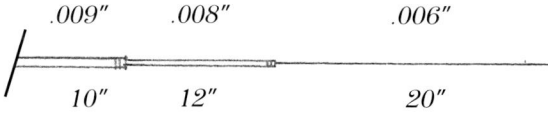

.009″   .008″   .006″

10″   12″   20″

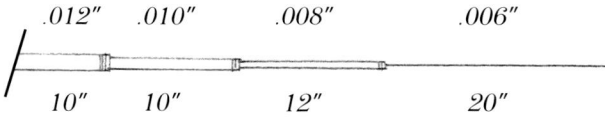

.012″   .010″   .008″   .006″

10″   10″   12″   20″

Dry Fly Leaders

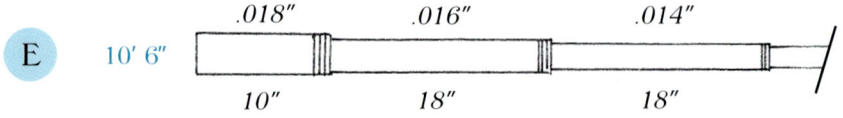

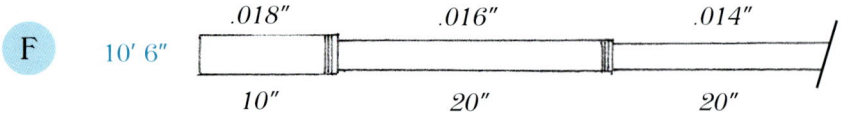

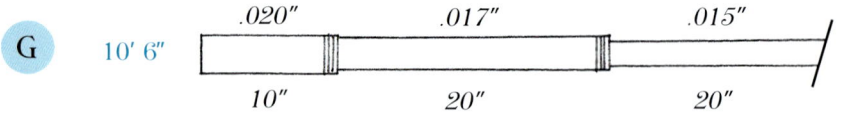

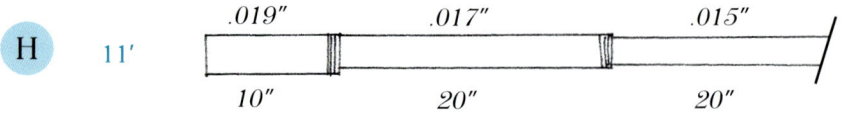

E 10' 6"

.018"　　　.016"　　　.014"

10"　　　18"　　　18"

F 10' 6"

.018"　　　.016"　　　.014"

10"　　　20"　　　20"

G 10' 6"

.020"　　　.017"　　　.015"

10"　　　20"　　　20"

H 11'

.019"　　　.017"　　　.015"

10"　　　20"　　　20"

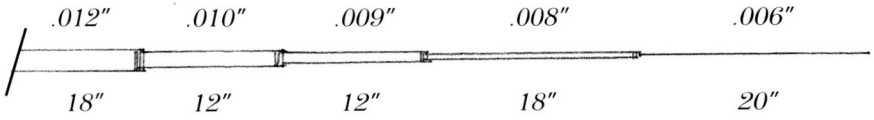

.012″ .010″ .009″ .008″ .006″

18″ 12″ 12″ 18″ 20″

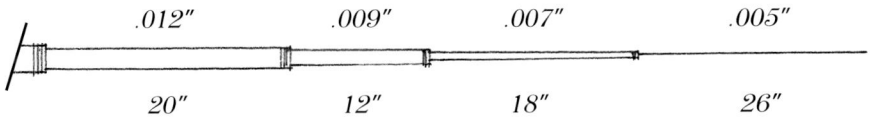

.012″ .009″ .007″ .005″

20″ 12″ 18″ 26″

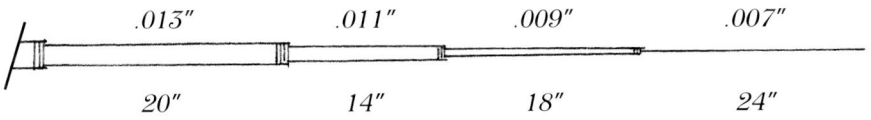

.013″ .011″ .009″ .007″

20″ 14″ 18″ 24″

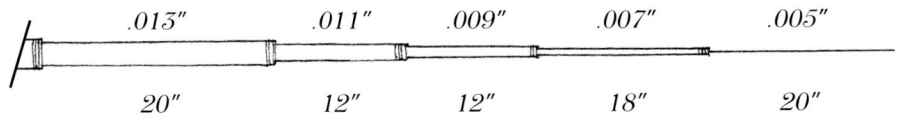

.013″ .011″ .009″ .007″ .005″

20″ 12″ 12″ 18″ 20″

Nymph/Wet Fly Leaders

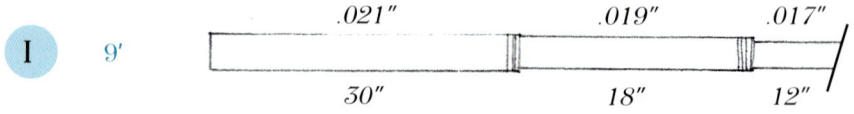

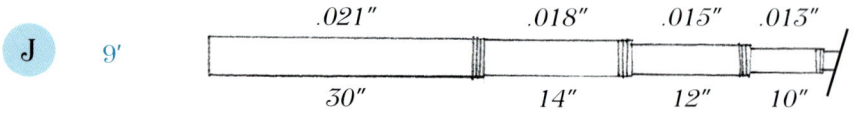

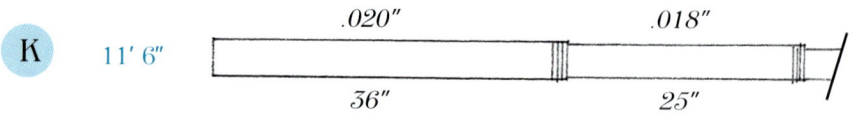

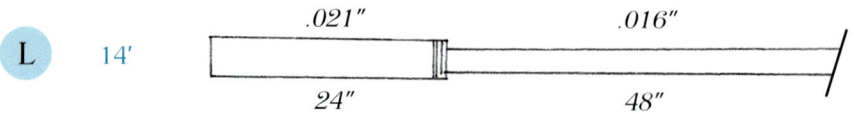

I 9'

.021"   .019"   .017"

30"   18"   12"

J 9'

.021"   .018"   .015"   .013"

30"   14"   12"   10"

K 11' 6"

.020"   .018"

36"   25"

L 14'

.021"   .016"

24"   48"

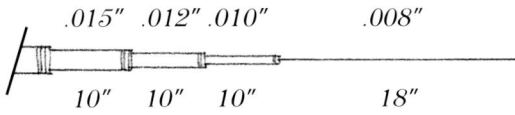

.015" .012" .010"   .008"

10"   10"   10"   18"

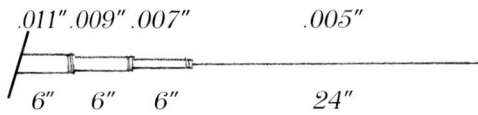

.011" .009" .007"   .005"

6"   6"   6"   24"

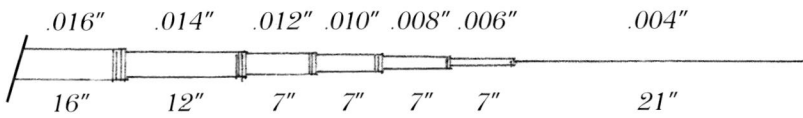

.016"   .014"   .012" .010" .008" .006"   .004"

16"   12"   7"   7"   7"   7"   21"

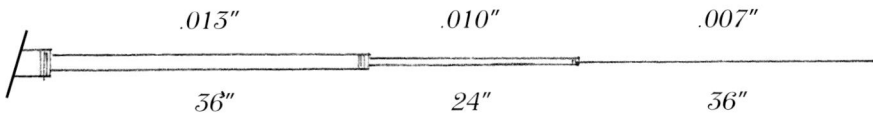

.013"   .010"   .007"

36"   24"   36"

Saltwater Leaders

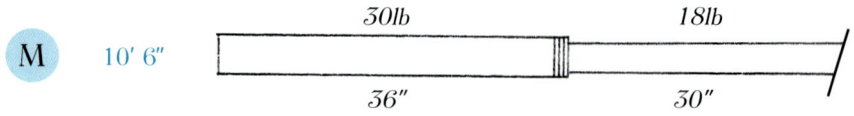

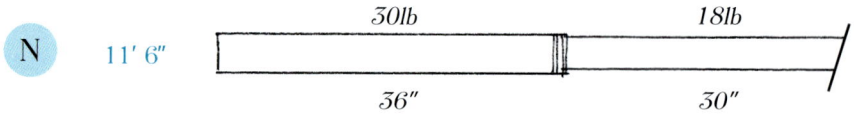

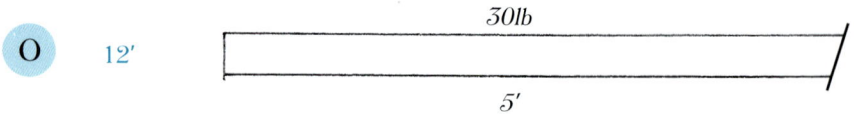

M   10' 6"

	30lb		18lb	
	36"		30"	

N   11' 6"

	30lb		18lb	
	36"		30"	

O   12'

30lb

5'

Heavy Saltwater Leader

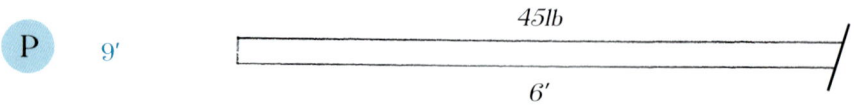

P   9'

45lb

6'

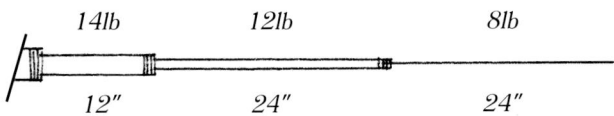

14lb   12lb   8lb

12"   24"   24"

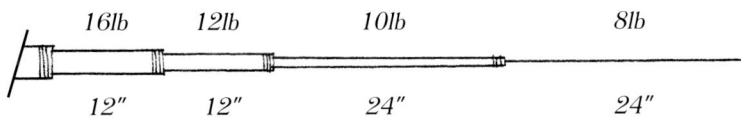

16lb   12lb   10lb   8lb

12"   12"   24"   24"

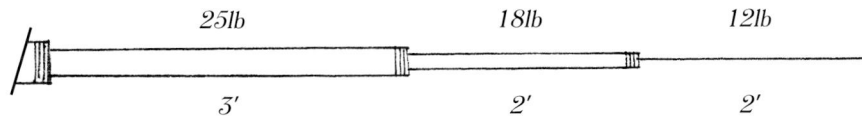

25lb   18lb   12lb

3'   2'   2'

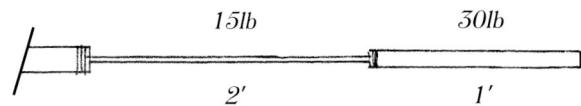

15lb   30lb

2'   1'

Saltwater Flats Leaders

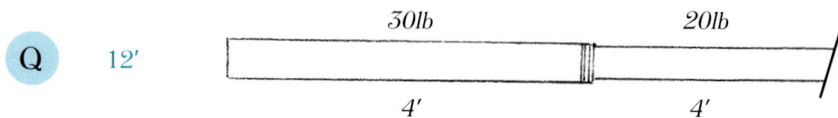

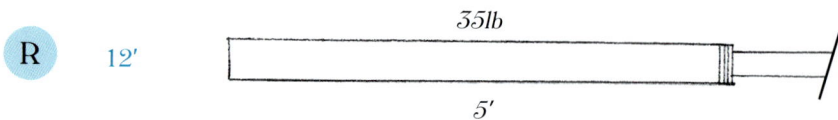

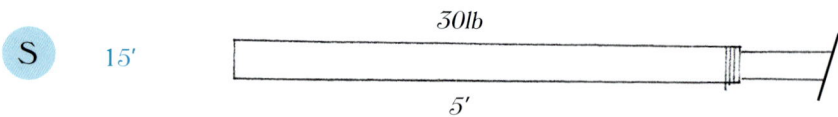

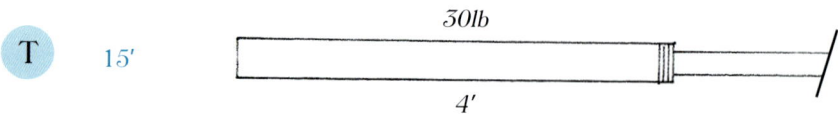

Q   12'

30lb   20lb

4'   4'

R   12'

35lb

5'

S   15'

30lb

5'

T   15'

30lb

4'

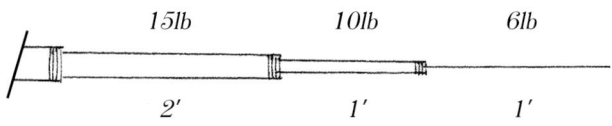

15lb   10lb   6lb

2'   1'   1'

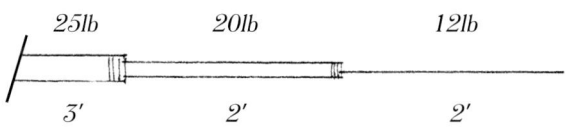

25lb 20lb   12lb

3'   2'   2'

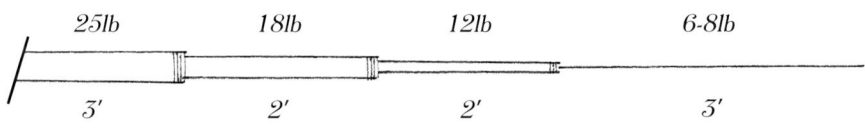

25lb   18lb   12lb   6-8lb

3'   2'   2'   3'

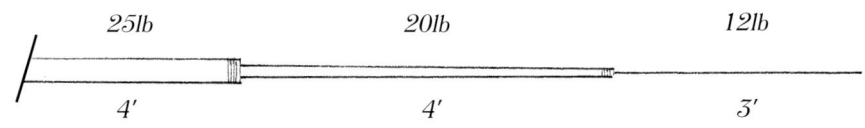

25lb   20lb   12lb

4'   4'   3'

Tying Notes

Tying Notes